CARMEN WARRINGTON

who am I?

Discover your inner world

who

CARMEN WARRINGTON

am I?

Discover your inner world

with illustrations by Linda Franklin

Lothian
BOOKS

Thomas C. Lothian Pty Ltd
132 Albert Road, South Melbourne, Victoria 3205
www.lothian.com.au

Text copyright © Carmen Warrington 2004
Illustrations copyright © Linda Franklin 2004
First published 2004

National Library of Australia
Cataloguing-in-Publication data:

Warrington, Carmen.
  Who am I?

  ISBN 0 7344 0591 X

  1. Self-help techniques. 2. Meditations.
  I. Franklin, Linda, 1963– . II. Title.

158.1

Designed by Kim Roberts Design
Edited by Magnolia Flora and Sue Harvey
Printed in Australia by Hyde Park Press

Carmen Warrington is the best-selling author of *Today I Will; 100 ways to make your life calm and creative*. She has studied the art of meditation with the Brahma Kumaris since 1984. Her internationally acclaimed meditation CDs have helped thousands of people around the world find inner peace and power.

Carmen performs gentle and uplifting Calm and Creative concerts with her partner David Jones. She conducts guided meditations at public events and through her Melbourne-based Calm and Creative business she runs workshops and consultations in self-awareness and meditation. Visit her website www.calmandcreative.com.au

Linda Franklin is a professional artist and art therapist who lives and exhibits her paintings on the Mornington Peninsula, Victoria. She facilitates workshops for clarity and wellbeing, exploring movement, sound, sculpture, image-making, affirmations and visualisations. For events and classes visit www.heartistry.com.au

who am I?

I am a **peace dove**

I am a **messenger** of peace. I don't convey my message through words, for the olive branch I carry would fall from my beak.

It is not through my actions that I convey my peace message, though I never use my wings to attack. My wings are for flight. From high above the Earth I can see that national boundaries do not really exist. Nothing truly separates one human being from another, and from my vantage point I can only marvel at the wonder of every living thing.

The **respect** I have for all life is the message of peace I bring.

I am spring

This is my time of new birth and new growth. Suddenly one day there is a feeling of vitality in the air, and everything awakens after a deep, nourishing sleep. It is a time of rapid growth, the blossoming of creative forces in full flight. My energy is fresh and exuberant. It is the time of excitement, wonder and optimism.

But if spring was eternal, with constant growth, I would become depleted of energy, exhausted. After new growth I need to sustain and develop what I have created. Slowly but surely, the cycle turns.

who am I?
I am a **traveller**

I am on a one-way journey. I left the starting point long ago and there's no turning back. My **destination** lies ahead, but to focus solely on the journey's end is to miss the gifts I am offered each step of the way. I have many travelling **companions** who stay with me until their own journey steers them on a different course — then we part company.

Whenever I face a major crossroad or obstacle, my guide is there to offer counsel. The path I take is dictated by my own **choices**, so my guide remains silent until I seek advice.

who am I?
I am a **bird in flight**

I was born with the gift of faith. My birthright is to soar high above the world. I can steer a course with the wind and enjoy the freedom of flight. I fly in **harmony** with my flock or experience the joyous **solitude** of my own company.

Desiring to be in the celestial blue, all I need do is leave my tree and fly, but sometimes doubts and fears keep me clinging to its branches. I have **faith** in the wind. I reaffirm my faith in myself and let go.

who am I?

I am an **actor**

In my lifelong career I play a variety of roles, many within a single day. Each role I assume requires a set of behaviours: a leader exercises authority, a team-member co-operates, a parent nurtures and guides, a counsellor listens intently, an agent for change challenges the way things are.

An actor's mastery lies in removing the previous role before beginning the next. The danger in being an actor is that I can lose myself in a role, and believe that I am the role I play.

At the end of the day, I remove all the trappings of the characters I have portrayed and come back to my essential self.

who am I?

I am a **buried treasure**

I contain riches beyond belief. I am rich in qualities, virtues, traits and talents, gifts that were inherited at birth and to which I have added value over a lifetime of experiences. Yet somehow the wealth within me remains hidden, and I believe that I am only worthless rocks and pebbles.

I have acquired many beliefs about myself from my society and my family. These beliefs may not have been imposed intentionally, but they weigh me down. I loosen the compacted soil of others' beliefs, bringing my treasure to the surface.

who am I?
I am a **mountain stream**

My journey begins high in the mountain peaks, where the atmosphere is **pure**, unpolluted by the trappings of daily life. Purity is my essence. My purpose is movement, and the downward slope entices me on an adventure to the ocean. Along the way I gather momentum and strength. Along the way I accumulate impurities, but I am not the rubbish I carry. Once I reach my destination I will **release** all impurities into the vast, purifying waters.

Recalling my **sweet**, clean essence, I filter out all the waste, all the negativity I have accumulated, and I experience my purity.

who am I?

I am an **infant**

I have a great passion to **learn**, and failure is an incentive for me to try again. I make progress through enthusiastic trial and error. Learning to walk is an **adventure**. I often fall, but I get up and try again and eventually succeed. And once I have mastered walking, I want to run!

I remain enthusiastic. I keep trying regardless of setbacks, not wanting to give up. I **encourage** myself: 'Keep going. Never mind if you fall, get up and try again. You can do it. We all make mistakes. You're doing well.'

I am a jewel

A jewel has no desire to be set in silver or gold, to be made into a necklace or a ring. The jewel is content no matter how the jeweller chooses to fashion its housing.

Even if I am hidden away in a drawer I know my own worth, my own beauty. My radiance remains constant. I don't need to be noticed to know my true value. In a world that reveres the illusion of fame and celebrity, I practise the art of self-appreciation. I am content with who I am, with what I have. I am content with my life.

who am I?

I am a **student**

I am a student in the school of life, taking a practical course in happiness. People, situations and events present me with **opportunities** for learning. Instead of asking 'Why me?', the student asks 'What is the lesson here?' I am in a class of my own, a class especially made for me. Until a lesson is learnt its circumstances will continue to recur, in a variety of shapes and forms. I may be given small tests or a major examination to chart my progress in the school of life.

To pass with honour, I work closely with my wise teacher, who encourages me to **discover** my own answers. In this way I gain lasting **wisdom**.

I am a **warrior**

I am a brave warrior. My task is simple: I must face the enemy with **courage**. I keep facing my enemies, never turning my back to run away. My enemies are the things that rob me of my peace and power. I know beyond doubt that no matter what the situation, no matter what the challenge, my enemy is within me. The enemy is not anything or anyone else, the enemy is my own weakness, my own shortcomings.

For every weakness in me I have an opposing **strength**. In **facing** my enemies I come to know which weapons will bring me victory.

who am I?

I am an **open palm**

I accept everything that life offers me. No opportunity is missed. I am able to **receive** the next gift because I have let go of the previous one.

Sometimes I hold on too tightly, afraid that no more gifts will come my way. By holding on I block other possibilities and I risk crushing what I hold so tightly in my clenched fist.

I **allow** all things to come and go, and **cherish** them while they are in my safekeeping.

who am I?

I am a **guest**

Being the guest, I am **carefree**. This is not my residence, and everything I use is a **gift** from my host. I am grateful for all that I receive. I appreciate even the smallest gestures of kindness, the simplest offerings. Nothing is taken for granted. Gratitude comes easily for a guest who is bestowed with many blessings while simply passing though life.

who am I?
I am a moonless night

There is no light in my dark sky. The way ahead is obscured and I relish the blackness. It is all I have and it consumes me.

The darkness and I become one. All that is dark in me arises: it longs to be known yet cannot abide the light, concealing itself in the presence of the moon. Sometimes, terrifying monsters emerge that I never knew were within me. They linger and prowl and make themselves known to me.

Touched by the new moon's first light the darkness vanishes, but I have felt it. Now that I recognise what lies within me, I can begin another cycle of self-transformation.

I am **summer**

This is my time of **abundance**. Success comes easily as I enjoy the flowers and **fruits** of my earlier labours. This is a time of fullness and expansion as I nurture and develop my new creations to their full potential. Youthful energy ripens into **maturity**.

But if summer was eternal, expansion would reach its limits and boredom or inertia would set in. After fullness, I desire to make some changes. Slowly but surely, the cycle turns.

who am I?
I am a
rechargeable battery

I am powerful, but my energy supply has limits: when I use it, I lose it. I am wise about what drains my energy and what empowers me. I can recharge easily, and how I recharge depends on what type of energy I want to replace. Physical energy requires physical **replenishment**, spiritual **energy** requires spiritual topping up.

An unlimited power source is always available to me. Whenever I want, I can plug into the source and fill my soul with as much power as I want.

I am a **reporter**

I have a passion for passing on what I see, hear or witness, but I never pass on what I **witness** without adding my own opinions. I shape the story to suit my purpose, and I am selective about what I report. I construct the story I want to tell by including and excluding certain pieces of information.

The question is, 'What is my **purpose** in reporting?' Is it to uplift or to stir up unrest? Or is my purpose to spread peace and **goodwill**? An important question I ask myself before I launch into my next report is 'Why am I telling this story?'

I am the **sea**

When the weather is calm my waves roll gently. When stormy winds blow I am wild and out of control. On the surface I am influenced by my surroundings. But I am also **deep**, and way down beneath my surface is another world. In my depths I have a mysterious and secret world of stillness, **silence**, beauty, hidden colour and great power.

Instead of dwelling on the surface where I interact with the world outside, I spend time visiting my depths so that I can become **resilient** to the winds of change.

who am I?
I am an instrument

The virtuoso musician makes beautiful music through me. The musician has **unlimited** creative power, but I am the means to express that well of **creativity**. Without me, the musician has only talent, but the **marriage** of player and instrument creates music. What music will be played through me today, and who shall accept the applause?

I am **autumn**

This is my time of **reflection** and **release**, for gathering and giving away. A cool change inspires me to harvest my creations and store for the future. What is unused decays, and what is not relevant is released. Change is in the air and I let go of what was, making way for what will be.

But if autumn was eternal, the sense of loss would be overwhelming; I might let go too much and be left with nothing. I need to make new plans and to create new dreams. Slowly but surely the cycle turns.

I am a **caretaker**

I came naked into this world, and when I leave I will take nothing with me, not even the body I call my own.

I have accumulated many objects around me. I have journeyed with many people. I do not own anything or anyone, not even my children. As a caretaker my duty is to **care** for that which is placed in my trust. I enjoy the things in my life, but my **enjoyment** does not depend on those things. To claim ownership is to be trapped in the material world, where I will be consumed by desires and suffer many hurts and disappointments. So I remain a **simple** caretaker.

who am I?

I am a **stick of incense**

Mysterious, other-worldly wafts of smoke curl through the air, circling, dreamily rising. I am releasing the smoke of my thoughts, my attitudes, my intentions, my feelings. Although these are **subtle**, they do have an effect. They permeate the atmosphere and influence the mood in the room.

If my thoughts are negative, my **attitude** less than generous and my intention destructive, I release a heavy, pungent odour. If my thoughts are kind, my attitude understanding and my intention to bring about benefit, my fragrant aroma **uplifts** the atmosphere.

I influence the atmosphere in subtle yet powerful ways.

I am a **star**

I've been put up here to be.

Not to do — to **be**.

Up here I am way beyond the cares and troubles of the world — I am **free** just to be. Free to radiate light, for my essence is light and peace. Anyone who looks up at the night sky can feel my peace. I am blissfully detached up here, removed from everything and everyone, but when I want to I can shoot down to earth, straight back to activity. I love the **simplicity** up here; the peace. Occasionally, it's good for the soul just to be.

who am I?

I am a **diamond**

I was once coal; black carbon buried deep underground. In the dark I have endured intense heat and borne incredible pressure. I have endured, and my **endurance** of pressure and heat has rearranged my molecules into the perfect structure of the diamond.

Now I am a jewel of great beauty, but I am not fragile or delicate. Thanks to the pressures I have learnt to **tolerate**, I am tough and **resilient** and can withstand many things without harming my essential beauty. My energy is not distracted by life's pressures, so I am free to play with the light.

I am a **raindrop**

who am I?

Compared to the ocean, a single raindrop seems insignificant, ridiculously small and inconsequential. But in the thirsty desert, a single raindrop is **precious**, life-giving and vitally important. To give something when and where it is needed is what really counts. Then it is a truly valued **gift**.

Is our world an ocean of peace or a desert? Even though I am only a single drop, every drop of **peace** counts. I do make a difference.

I am the moon

I run playful circles around the Earth, but I have a love affair with the Sun. The Earth is the world with which I interact, for it is where my light falls, but the Sun is the source of my light. I play a game with the Sun, orbiting the playing field of Earth, while keeping my face to the Sun.

The dance of life takes the three of us into many configurations. Sometimes the Earth stands between me and my beloved Sun and I fall into darkness. Sometimes I am completely bathed in sunlight and the Earth enjoys my radiant fullness. What a dance! What a game of waxing and waning light! What bliss when I am fully facing the Sun.

who am I?
I am a mountain climber

Exhilaration fills my lungs as I make my way up the slope, fuelled by the prospect of attaining the peak. Conditions are harsh and the weather conspires against me. As the difficulties mount, the small voice that was urging me to turn back yells in my face 'Give up!' But the dream won't go away and my **determination** increases. I discover the meaning of **perseverance** as I push myself higher, until finally I am at the top. I've done it. The view from up here is intoxicating.

In the distance a higher peak captures my imagination; before the descent is over I am dreaming again.

who am I?
I am a
jewel-trader

I deal in precious gems; I don't waste my time with worthless rocks. I have learnt to tell the difference, sometimes the hard way. People cheated me, and I took their fakes in good faith. Each mistake honed my eye, sharpened my wits, and refined my ability to discern what is of value. I trust more and more in my intuition, and can sense what is true and what is false.

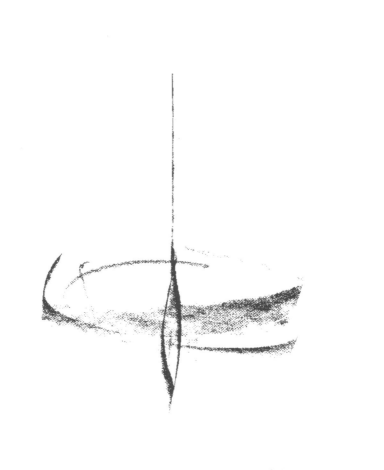

who am I?

I am a
pendulum

I seek **balance**, always. In my quest I swing from one side to the other, sometimes wildly, and seemingly out of control. I must explore both extremes and all points in between or I will be pulled later to what I have not already investigated.

The still centre, which I crave, is the result of visiting all **possibilities**, all extremes.

who am I?

I am a **butterfly**

At present I am in my cocoon, but I was born to be a butterfly. With time and the **nurturing** warmth of the sun, I will fulfill my destiny. For now I dream of my true colours. I dream of flight and of a beautiful field of flowers in which I will dance. Transformation is **inevitable**. In fact, **transformation** is under way. I focus on my beautiful future; my patience will be rewarded.

who am I?

I am an **elastic band**

When nothing is bothering me, I am relaxed. Then something comes along and gets under my skin. I hook onto it and it pulls me out of my peaceful state. It tugs me, it pulls me, it stretches me to the point of tension, until I think I will break.

All I have to do is let it go with my mind. It is not holding onto me, I am holding onto it. If I don't hold onto it anymore, I will instantly snap back to my former shape.

who am I?

I am a **cloud**

My life revolves around giving, but it never feels like a burden. I relax. I float in the sky. I am light and easy. I have no need to rush, no need to do anything.

When I have rested, the sun coaxes me to gather water from the ocean and fill myself with life-giving droplets of rain. I fill myself up before I give to others. This is a kind of self-service. When I am a full rain cloud, I shower my contents onto the thirsty earth.

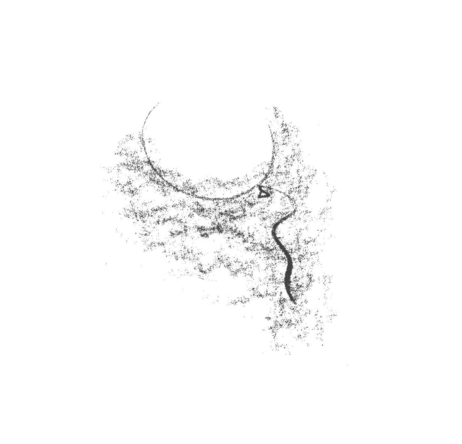

I am a balloon

I was born to **celebrate**. I am a reminder that an ordinary event can be a celebration of life. I am filled with the breath of happiness. I am light and joyful and buoyant.

My happiness has nothing to do with the world outside. Nothing outside me can destroy my happiness. If my happiness diminishes it is because the air is leaking out of me. I attend to my weaknesses and **repair** any holes so that my **happiness** remains intact.

who am I?

I am a
superhero

I am fulfilled when I can be of service to humanity. I have a special **ability** that was given to me at birth. Sometimes it takes all my ingenuity to work out how my **power** will help in a particular situation.

Sometimes I forget that I am a superhero and believe I am just an ordinary mortal. At these times it is impossible to access my super-power. To use my power I simply **remember** who I am and what I have to offer the world.

who am I?
I am a **magnet**

Who I **believe** I am has a more powerful influence over me than who I am. Each belief I hold carries a magnetic field that draws a similar energy towards me. The more **conviction** I have that a belief is true, the more powerful is its magnetic pull.

If I believe I am lucky, good fortune is attracted to me. If I believe I deserve to be treated badly, I attract abusive relationships. If I believe I am nothing special, I **attract** experiences in which I become invisible. My worst fears and my greatest hopes are magnetically attracting experiences to me. It is time to review the beliefs I hold about myself.

I am a **garden**

I am full of life, beautiful life. I flourish and grow through many seasons, enjoying ever-changing blazes of colour and shape in buds, blossoms, flowers, berries, leaves, trees and grasses. I give great joy and pleasure to the gardener.

Of course, I have some weeds. I am a garden, and every living thing finds expression in me. I feel no shame about my weeds. They are natural, and the gardener will tend to them when the time is right, for timing is an important aspect of the gardener's work. I am proud of who I am. If I only see my weeds, I cannot appreciate the beauty of all my luxurious flowers and shrubs, or the majesty of each tree.

I am a **block of ice**

I am brittle, static and unyielding. Something triggered a painful reaction in me and the only way I could cope was to shut down. My ability to love has frozen over. Bitter cold winds blow across my words and people slip and slide on my frosty intentions. I am icy cold and uninviting.

Fortunately, this state is not permanent and a simple remedy exists. I apply warmth. I will melt, and love will flow again. If I start to warm from inside me, my heart will thaw more quickly.

who am I?
I am a bushfire

An incident set off a spark, a reaction in me that ignited my anger. How small was that spark and how all-consuming and out of control is the fire that blazes now.

The truth is that the land was dry, the trees were parched, primed for another fire to flare. The terrain was still smoking, the embers still smouldering from an earlier outburst.

I am on the rampage now, devouring everything in my path; but while I am consumed with fury I can't stop the inferno. I will have deep regrets later, but my passionate outburst is unstoppable. People are avoiding me — they don't want to get burnt. If only the rain would come. Cool reason will save me. Understanding will moisten the land and prevent this destructive rage from re-igniting.

I am an earthquake

who am I?

Down in the core of my being, major shifts are taking place. I am **redefining** myself at the deepest level and nothing will ever be the same again. When the **foundation** rearranges itself, everything built upon it becomes unstable. Up on the surface, there is upheaval of catastrophic proportions. Life is completely disrupted, alarms are sounding and damage control is the only way ahead until the shaking stops.

The quaking ground frightens people, but I could not go on as things were. My deeply suppressed needs are surfacing and must be dealt with. As I learn to respond to my **needs** rather than burying them, the frequency of these massive disruptions will decrease.

I am a lake

I am shapeless water. My nature is fluid; I adapt according to my needs. Whatever my surroundings are, I take on their shape. My way is not to resist but to surrender to the circumstances of the moment. I do not force things to be the way I want them to be, but go with the flow. This is the source of my serenity. In surrendering to the way things are I find stillness. Freed from upheaval and resistance, I am at peace.

I am a **rock**

I am solid rock. My nature is enduring; I stay **true** to myself no matter what changes occur around me. I protect the way things are. I am not seduced by novelty. I respect the past and won't abandon it without good reason.

I am **strong** and resistant, but not stubborn. I can be moulded. Over time I can be shaped by water. **Patience** is my great virtue, the secret to my inner peace.

who am I?
I am an
alchemist

I have mastered the art of transforming something worthless into something **priceless**. I can turn lead into gold.

The artistry of transformation is in my perception. The secret is to see the innate value of everything. **Respect** things for what they are and they become gold.

The same applies to people. Each person on this Earth is part of God's creation, and who am I to doubt their worth? The alchemy is to focus on the pure gold within each one. This takes great determination, but my pure heart and my **divine vision** are strong enough to overlook the visible lead and seek the hidden gold.

who am I?

I am a bridge-builder

Once there was a single land, but now there are many isolated islands, surrounded by the waters of my tears. I separated myself from people with whom I shared toxic **relationships** in the past.

To recover my sense of **wholeness** and wellbeing, I choose to make links between the islands. Not for those people to re-enter my life, but for me to revisit my past with wisdom and understanding. I own my part in allowing, accepting and prolonging their poisonous behaviour. I own any unfair expectations I placed upon them. I open my heart and **forgive**. I build bridges to heal the rifts in my soul.

who am I?

I am an
hourglass

The master of time has filled my upper chamber with sand; until every grain has trickled into the lower chamber I must be **patient**. Nothing can hurry or interfere with divine timing.

Each task, each project, each lesson, each process is subject to divine timing. I am learning to live fully in the **present** as I contemplate each grain passing through the narrow neck and into its place below. The grains fall second by second, moment by moment.

I am a **feather**

The winds of destiny summon me to my future and my **journey** continues. I float blissfully along on **gentle** breezes and upward-spiralling currents of warm air. Sometimes a strong gust catches me unaware, propelling me into the unknown. At other times I lie inert where I have been dumped by violent, battering winds.

A feather has no power to resist the force of the winds. I must simply remain light so that my landing will be painless. My **lightness** of being allows me to catch hold of even a slight puff of wind, so that I can follow my destiny.

who am I?

I am a **rose-bush**

My talent is to **bloom** with perfumed flowers. I give immense pleasure to anyone who chances upon my exquisite roses. My thorns are equally renowned. They are my defence. If I am frightened because someone is getting too close, my thorns pierce their tender skin and they recoil from me.

But not everyone who approaches me will hurt me. Most people just want to come close to my flowers and enjoy their lovely fragrance. Sharing my gifts is good for both of us. With **courage** I learn to **trust** and to communicate my needs.

who am I?

I am a **sparrow**

I am a **humble** creature with no particular claim to fame. I am not powerful like the eagle, colourful like the parrot or majestic like the peacock. I am small and plain, indistinguishable from other sparrows.

Yet every morning I announce the dawn. And I don't just whisper, I **sing** my heart out. Although it's possible that not a single creature will hear my song, I simply use the talents I was given.

My strength lies in my self-worth. I'm **happy** with who I am. I don't long to swap places with the eagle, the parrot or the peacock. And I am fortunate: I am the first creature **kissed** by the rays of the sun each morning.

I am a **storm**

My thunderous words and flashes of lightning are intended to hurt, but my aim is poor because of all the tears I rain down, so no real harm is done. My tears tell the **truth** of my stormy outburst — I am hurting inside.

I **retreat** to my calm centre. It's called the eye of the storm because this is where I look at myself to discover what the turmoil is about. The storm has been brewing for a while. Why did I let it build to this intensity? What am I really feeling? What am I expecting? What have I not communicated?

The damage report is substantial, but at least the air is **clear** and the atmosphere is not so heavy.

who am I?

I am an **artist**

I express things creatively, the way I see them. If a dozen artists paint the same scene, there will be a dozen different images. How can I say that one version is right or wrong, better or worse than another? Surely it's all a matter of perception.

I see things from a certain angle, with a particular focus. I compose my picture according to my tastes, my intentions. I imbue with meaning and significance all the objects, characters and events that I depict. More importantly, I appreciate that we are all artists, each enjoying our own perspective on life. I honour your perceptions as much as my own.

I am a **tree**

I extend my branches in a joyful gesture, celebrating life. What a **vibrant** and diverse existence this is. I bear the branches of work, family, friends, health, dreams, ambitions. Each branch divides into limbs and twigs; the expansion is astonishing. My **life-force** pulses through each branch to every single leaf.

And to think I was once just a tiny seed.

When I am overwhelmed by it all, when I wonder how I send my energy to each twig and leaf, I remember the seed. When I concentrate on my **essence**, I am revitalised.

who am I?
I am a **puppet-master**

I acquired this exquisite living puppet a long time ago, and practised for years to bring it completely under my control. Now I carry out complex actions with great artistry, as if the puppet and I are one. It obeys my will and responds to my subtlest intentions.

But I am not the puppet. There is a story to be enacted, written in the pages of destiny. The mastery lies in being unaffected by that story, simply remaining an observer as the drama unfolds, without losing myself in strong emotions. I remain the master and I do not take things personally.

who am I?

I am a **fence**

I mark definite boundaries, so people know how far they can go. It's up to me to decide what is private and what is public property. These **boundaries** can change according to the circumstances; it is my responsibility to ensure that they are clearly defined.

But a fence is not a brick wall, and there are many gates dotted along the perimeter. If you seek my **permission**, then you may be **welcome** to enter. However, I reserve the right to say no. All I ask is that you respect my boundaries.

I am an **archer**

My **thoughts** are arrows, and every arrow I release reaches its target. Once an arrow is shot, it cannot be recalled.

Sometimes I play the part of Cupid and my loving thoughts arrive as **blessings** to the receiver. Sometimes I am a warrior and I mean to wound the enemy. The most dangerous thoughts are those that reach their target on poison-tipped arrows. These are the poisonous thoughts of jealousy, rage, bitterness, resentment and hatred. The poisonous thoughts are doubly damaging for they affect the sender as much as the receiver. To avoid injuring myself I remain **aware** of the quality of my thoughts.

who am I?
I am **winter**

This is my time of withdrawal and recovery. I **rest** deeply and **regenerate**. I survive underground with what I have stored and save my energy for introspection. I think, reflect, question. I put things in perspective. I seek new directions and sow the seeds of new ideas. This is the season of gestation, between conception and birth, and nothing is apparent yet.

But if winter was eternal, the unfulfilled potential of new seeds would be unbearable. Life must go on; slowly but surely the **cycle** turns.

I am a **driver**

This body is a **luxury** vehicle that I drive, and all the sense organs are designed to give me maximum **pleasure** as I travel.

Apart from refuelling, I need to attend to ongoing maintenance. If I don't fix little problems, one day I'll have to take the car off the road for major repairs.

Sometimes my mind is preoccupied and I drive on automatic pilot. That's when habit takes over and I end up in the wrong place. Or accidents occur as I say things I didn't intend, crashing into others' feelings. While driving, I must remain fully conscious, fully **aware**.

who am I?

I am a **sunset**

Only a certain amount can be achieved in a single day. I am a reminder that **patience** is needed, and that taking a break is a necessary part of any process. Putting things to rest graciously, I celebrate with a **splendid** show of light. I honour the day's end and mark the passing of that day into history. The past is now past. I celebrate every single day, not just the days when a great success is achieved. I honour the fact that every day is a victory. I **shine** light onto all the events of the day, and I find much to be grateful for.

I am a **scientist**

My special research is to discover all about myself and find out how I function best. My method is scientific; it begins with impartial **observation**. I remain detached from the findings, a mere observer. I study my outward behaviour and its results.

Under the microscope of my awareness I study the subtle energies of my thoughts and feelings. From my observations I formulate theories, which I test through **experimentation**. If I think like this, how will it make me feel? What will the outcome be? What if I make a subtle change? In this way I become an expert in my subject — the self.

I am a **knight**

I am the Lord of my castle, and no one shall conquer me. I have built myself an impenetrable fortress of **protection**, surrounded by a moat. The drawbridge to my castle will **open** only when I give the command. I've encased myself in a suit of armour — nobody can hurt me now. It's a shame I'm so hard to embrace with these metal limbs.

I am **safe**, but at what cost? Is it just the enemy I am keeping out?

I am a **lotus**

I am celebrated for my **pure** white petals and radiant beauty. People think I have a blessed and fortunate existence, floating on the surface of the water having nothing to do with the gritty realities of life in the dirt. Perhaps they don't realise my feet are firmly rooted in the slimy mud. I am well and truly **grounded** in this earthly plane.

What keeps me above it all? It's not the water; I don't rely on my surroundings to hold me up. What keeps me afloat is the **peace** of mind I receive from breathing the clean, pure air, and the power I receive from the light of the sun.

who am I?

I am a **blank page**

My story has been written up to this page — the **present** moment. The main characters have entered; events have unfolded; themes have been introduced and developed. All this influences the next page in my story.

A blank page is **powerful** because its potential is truly unlimited. Anything can happen now. My story could take a twist and a whole new chapter might begin. The past, although imprinted deeply in the previous pages, has truly passed. This blank page offers **freedom** from the way things have been. Where will I take my story now?

I am a spider

I weave a wonderful web for myself, drawing all the threads of my life together as one. I move freely around the web, tending to the different aspects of my world.

When I feel needy, insecure or unsure of myself my web becomes sticky, binding everything tightly. My web of attachments traps everything including myself, weighing down my world. One day the web I've spun could collapse under the strain.

I engage in a healthy interaction with the world without becoming trapped. I free myself from attachment to many things: places, possessions, people, opinions; the way I like things done; the way things once were and the way they ought to be. My freedom enables me to fill my world with love.

who am I?
I am a
snowflake

I am made of the same chemistry as all other snowflakes, but I am shaped by my particular journey through the elements, which gives me a **unique** identity.

Each snowflake is as **beautiful** as it is individual. There is no arrogance in my beauty and individuality; it is the wonder of nature. No snowflake is better than another — we are without competition. But each snowflake is more beautiful than the one before.

who am I?

I am a loudspeaker

I have no on-off switch; I am on continuous broadcast.
Whatever is going on inside me is transmitting loud and
clear into the immediate environment.

My soul is being projected into the external world. The
words I say are just sounds. The actions I perform are
simply movement. The real messages coming through the
loudspeaker are my thoughts, feelings and intentions.
I pay attention to my inner world, doing everything I can
to sweeten the music of my soul.

who am I?
I am a **sunrise**

The dark night — the domain of dreams and inertia —
is over. I herald the new day, where dreams are fulfilled.
I offer unlimited opportunities for experiencing love, peace
and happiness. A new day is dawning, and it's going to be
wonderful. Nothing need ever be the same again. My rosy
pink optimism dispels the darkness and my golden
enthusiasm invites the sky to display its vast
spaciousness where anything is possible. With such a
spectacular start it's going to be a beautiful day.

who am I?

I am an
ecosystem

My natural instinct is to survive; my ability to adapt enables me to do so. I respond and adjust to the many changes that occur in me, both internally and externally.

Above my instinct for survival, I have the will to thrive and **flourish**. For this I need to maintain the good health of my entire system. All of my parts, the sub-systems that make up my whole, depend upon the proper functioning of my other parts. It's a delicate **balance**. Each system must be given attention and energy in order that the whole flourishes. If even one system is not healthy it will undermine the **wellbeing** of the whole.

who am I?
I am a **tortoise**

What a speedy world. It's exhilarating, but oh, the mad acceleration of it all! If I had to go any faster, I think I might expire. I can only do so much. But what I do, I do well and with great **concentration**, one thing at a time.

Here's how I cope with all the demands on me. Whenever things are getting on top of me, I stop what I am doing and withdraw into my shell. Here I **centre** myself and remember my natural pace. This keeps me sane, and when I am **refreshed** I go back into the day.

who am I?

I am a
chameleon

I am very responsive to what is going on around me and I am coloured by the company I keep. My talent is to **blend** and **harmonise** with whatever and whoever I am near. I love mingling with other energies and letting them bring out all the varying shades of my personality. It's a great joy for me to **express** all the different colours of my being. And what are my true colours? All of them are me.

who am I?

I am a **dragon**

I am a **powerful** and formidable creature, a watchful guardian of one of the world's greatest treasures. The treasure chest I guard so closely contains my **self-worth**.

My wings carry me above any insults hurled my way. Insults, put-downs and abusive words are dispersed by the beating of my wings.

And the fire that I breathe? The fire is for burning any self-destructive words coming from my own mouth.

I am a caged lion

I used to roam the wilderness and knew no fear. But I allowed myself to be trapped in a cage of limitations. I prowl the cage, frightening onlookers with my pent-up frustration. Otherwise I mope around depressed and in a daze. How did I get caught? Perhaps I walked in freely, lured by the promise of an easy life?

I dream of running wild under the open sky. I still sense my **potential** for a free and **magnificent** life. I reassess my options: comfort or adventure; predictability or newness; familiarity or **exhilaration**? When I am ready to step out of the cage I will find that the door was never locked.

who am I?
I am an **athlete**

My **goal** is to maintain **peak** performance and to reach my personal best. The only person I am competing with is me. I keep my sights clearly on my goal and go for it. There are some things I can't do, or can't have, but when I focus on my goal, these things do not concern me.

There is no room for doubt — visualising myself as successful is the key. Setbacks, off-days and disappointments are all stepping stones to my **success**.

who am I?

I am a **movie star**

In the story of my life I play the lead role. I have roles in many other stories as well as the one in which I star. In some stories I play a **supporting** role; in others I am one of the extras.

Not every scene is about me. When it is someone else's scene, I try not to draw the **focus** towards myself. I keep my **opinions** in check — this is their scene and they are playing it their own way.

If invited, I give my opinion. Otherwise I refrain from adding to the mass of opinions already out there, even in thought. This leaves me free to concentrate on what I am doing.

I am a filter

I keep wasteful and harmful impurities from entering the terrain of my mind. It's a huge undertaking: input comes at me from all directions — from my own subconscious, from other people, and incessantly from the media.

Some impurities are subtle and slip through without me noticing them. Frequently I am misinformed about the effect of particular types of thoughts. I mistakenly let these thoughts through because I don't understand their impact on me. After a build-up of these negative thoughts the damage becomes apparent; I become more diligent about what I allow to filter into my mind.

who am I?

I am a
passenger

My boat is making its way to the opposite shore under the expert handling of the boatman. I sit back, relax, and enjoy the ride. But the passage is not always smooth. When rough waters rock the boat I panic and try to take control, and in the attempt I risk capsizing the vessel. The wisest course of action is to remain calm and trust the boatman to take me safely across the waters. I am in good hands.

who am I?

I am a **swan**

People say I am **special**: beautiful, noble and graceful. Really, I'm no more special than any other being.

Beautiful? I could complain that I'm too big, my neck is ridiculously long and my feathers are plain white. Graceful? I move through the water with ease, but my wings have been clipped and I can't fly.

In fact, I am special because without any arrogance I choose to see my **virtues**, not my shortcomings. I'm admired because I **accept myself** and enjoy the grace and beauty of who I am.

I am a **projector**

I consciously project an image of myself that I want the world to see. At the same time I unconsciously project an image of the real me. The result is a blurry double-image, and people can't quite make out who I am. They are confused by the two versions superimposed upon each other.

When I am honest and reveal my true self, when I am the same inside and out, my image comes sharply into focus. Then I can be seen clearly, and my relationships are far more real and beautiful.

who am I?

I am a **torch-bearer**

I can shine my light or allow the darkness to remain. It's a simple choice — on or off. In the light I see what is real, in the darkness imagination and fear take over. Fear causes me to view your actions with suspicion and think the worst of you.

Then I curse you with harsh judgements and critical opinions. I could bless you back into the light with my good wishes and pure feelings — no matter what you have done. Shall I plunge us both into darkness or into the light? The choice is mine and it's all in the flick of a switch.

I am a pearl

I was born of mere sand, yet I have a lustre that is highly prized. Without the intense chafing of that single grain of sand I would not be a pearl. The practice of dealing with **constant** irritations has created layer upon layer of my pearly beauty. There's **benefit** in everything.

Irritants will always be around, but what will I make of them? Will they remain gritty and annoying, or will I create more layers of pearl?

I am a key

I hold the power to release the captive mind from its self-imposed prison. I've been here all along, forgotten in the shadowy recesses of shame. I've become rusty through many tears of regret, bitterness and sorrow.

I am the key and I am love. To open the lock I need to be turned twice. Once for **acceptance**; I accept whatever I said or did as a necessary part of my growth, no matter how foolish or selfish I may have been. The second turn is for **forgiveness**; I don't need to punish myself any more. **Love** is the key.

I am a mandala

I am a mandala, a central point radiating outwards. My power lies in the centre — it is the source of all I am, and all I am capable of being.

The whole world is a mandala. From the solar system to an atom, the pattern of a central energy source surrounded by circles of energy is repeated endlessly.

Just like ripples on a lake, my thoughts and emotions permeate to the farthest reaches of my world, affecting each layer they pass through. Whenever I feel fragmented or spun out I bring my attention back to my centre, the source of my power.

who am I?

I am

I am **perfect** as I am, whatever I am.